FIRE TRUCKS

American fire fighters on the street

Photography by Henry Rasmussen

Motorbooks International
Publishers & Wholesalers Inc
Osceola, Wisconsin 54020, USA

First published in 1987 by Motorbooks International Publishers & Wholesalers Inc., PO Box 2, 729 Prospect Avenue, Osceola, WI 54020 USA

Motorbooks International is a certified trademark, registered with the United States Patent Office

Printed and bound in Hong Kong

The information in this book is true and complete to the best of our knowledge. All recommendations are made without any guarantee on the part of the author or publisher, who also disclaim any liability incurred in connection with the use of this data or specific details

Library of Congress Cataloging-in-Publication Data
Rasmussen, Henry
  Fire trucks.
    1. Fire-engines—United States—Pictorial works.
I. Title.
TH9371.R37   1987   628.9'25   87-14101
ISBN 0-87938-248-1

Motorbooks International books are also available at discounts in bulk quantity for industrial or sales-promotional use. For details write to Special Sales Manager at the Publisher's address

On the cover: This 1937 Pirsch equipage creates an appealing picture of fire engine grandeur.
On the back cover: This scene, showing the hind quarter of a 1950 Autocar, features fire-fighter gear from the fifties. **On the frontispiece:** The siren often receives attention over and above duty, as exemplified by this photograph of a polished-to-perfection unit, manufactured by the Federal Sign & Signal Corporation of Blue Island, Illinois. **On the title page:** The long hood, together with the rakish angle of the windshield and the open-air milieu of the doorless cockpit, imparts sports car characteristics to the 1937 White. **On this page:** Heavy-duty rubber is the focus in this picture, with its massive Firestone Transport tire and its bulky pair of fire-fighter boots. **On the next page:** Pride in the machinery is reflected in the gold leaf script decorating the hood of this classic Pirsch.

Contents

A proud heritage

The element of fire is older than civilization itself. Consequently, man has lived with this force since the beginning of time, gradually learning to take advantage of its beneficial possibilities, and simultaneously inventing better and ever more spectacular ways to combat its destructive characteristics—although these innovations, seen from a historic perspective, were indeed extremely slow in coming.

The Egyptians were known to have constructed pumps to fight fires. And the Romans formed fire-fighting brigades. But the advances made by these civilizations seem to have been lost with their demise. References to various inventions do appear in historic documents, however. The first hoses, for instance, were made from oxen entrails.

But generally it seems that the folks of those days fought an uphill battle, resigned to employing only the most primitive of processes. Thus, the good old "bucket brigade" constituted the universal method for hundreds of years. Although there are records of a variety of squirts and syringes and pumps, it was not until the middle of the seventeenth century—in Germany and England—that hand pumps appeared.

The earliest such contraption, built in England, arrived in America in 1731. The first hand pumpers constructed on this continent soon began to appear, but it would take another century before muscle power would be effectively replaced by steam power. Moses Latta of Cincinnati built a ten-ton monster in 1852. This city, the following year, also saw the formation of the first salaried fire fighters.

While steam power was used to operate the pump, horse power was still utilized for the transportation of the engine. The horse-drawn steam engines formed a picturesque part of the scenery for many decades, in some cases as late as the early twenties. The first unit both powered and propelled by a combustion engine arrived in the early part of the twentieth century, with Waterous introducing its version in 1906. Within a few years many of the pioneers, names such as American La France and Seagrave and Mack, had entered the market with products that would advance fire fighting another giant step.

Although certainly colorful and intriguing, the beautifully decorated contraptions from 100 years ago and more—the hand pumpers and the steam pumpers—belong to another era, an era than naturally forms a foundation for all the advances we see today, but one that is now far removed from that of the self-propelled era. This, and the fact that a book must have its limitations, constitute reasons for concentrating on the field of motorized fire engines.

Even with this set parameter, the field is frustratingly broad and impossible to cover in this fairly confined space. However, the viewer and reader will certainly be able to feel the nostalgia emanating from the beautiful and charming and awesome machines appearing on these pages. Many of the enthusiasts thumbing through this book will be fire fighters themselves, and will have a deep personal involvement with the equipment, as well as an awareness of the proud heritage of both the machines and the men who have made it their vocation to fight alongside them.

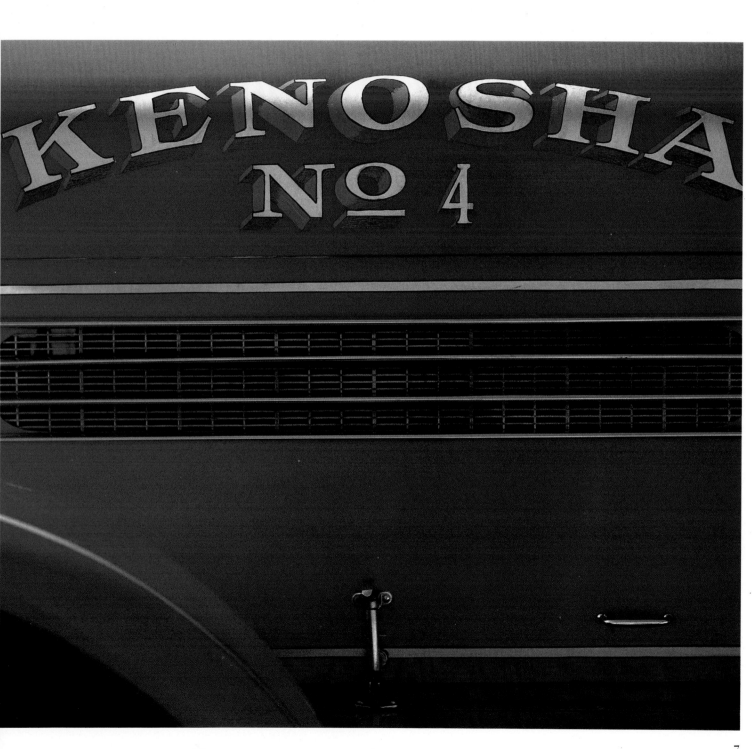

Ahrens-Fox

No other marque can match the reputation of Ahrens-Fox. The fame of this classic among classics must be attributed to a combination of performance and looks, with both aspects originating from the same feature—the piston pump. Numerous are the stories of its power, with one of the first accounts stemming from a demonstration in 1917, when an Ahrens-Fox elevated a stream of water as high as the Woolworth building in New York. And the looks, well, that maze of pipes and valves and gauges, crowned by that shining ball—all mounted up front— was a first-rate attention getter.

Chris Ahrens, of Cincinnati, Ohio, began manufacturing steam-operated fire engines already in 1869. After a series of mergers, which saw the formation of American La France in 1903, the founder retired. His sons and sons-in-law continued in the firm, but in 1904 decided to start their own. Charles Fox—one of the sons-in-law—became its president in 1910, at which time the classic double name was born.

Ahrens-Fox showed a steady growth through the next two decades, reaching a peak in 1928. But the Great Depression dealt the company a blow from which it never recovered. Only four units were built in 1934, and by 1936 a new owner had taken over. A series of subsequent owners kept production going on-and-off, until 1952 saw the completion of the last of the piston pumpers. Soon the proud name was dead.

The 1930 model featured here is one of the most outstanding in existence. The never-restored beauty is the pride of the Hall of Flame fire-fighting museum in Phoenix, Arizona.

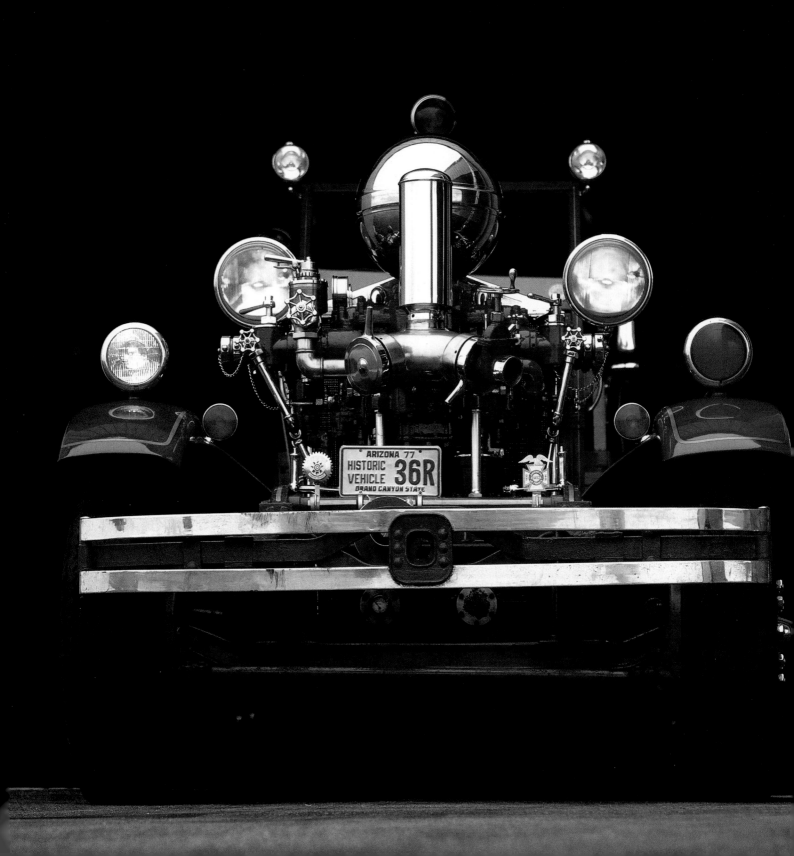

The photograph to the left shows the awesome face of the Ahrens-Fox with its front-mounted piston pump. The manufacturer supplied units with up to six cylinders—this example boasts the ultimate number, and produces 1,000 gpm (gallons per minute). The most eye-catching element of the pump is the ball-shaped surge tank, which performed the task of equalizing the water pressure on the pump side. On the hose side, the same task was performed by the cylindrical tank mounted just ahead of the ball unit.

Ahrens-Fox manufactured not only its own pumps and engines, but also its own axles, clutches, transmissions and bodies. In the photograph above and in the one on the following spread, the hood has been opened to reveal the potent power source. The six-cylinder unit has a displacement of 998 ci, a bore and stroke of 5.5×7 inches, and produces 110 hp. Wheelbase is a most impressive 22 ft. Overall length is 33 ft. Suspension is by semi-elliptical leaf springs front and rear. The smaller of the two tanks is

located behind the seat and holds fuel, while the larger holds water— 100 gal. One much appreciated that a feature of the front-mounted pump was the ease with which it could be maneuvered close to the water hydrant. But, while there was no disputing the many advantages of the piston pump, the complicated mechanism and the resulting higher cost of manufacture and maintenance caused its ultimate demise.

This bird's-eye view focuses on the Ahrens-Fox cockpit. Everything is heavy-duty here, beginning with the steering wheel, which boasts no less than five spokes—perhaps necessary, considering the effort required to turn it. Notice that the classic fire engine, like the classic racing car, featured right-hand drive. Mounted on the column are, on the left, the spark and throttle controls, and on the right, the add-on turn-signal lever. The two out-board levers operate the three-spread transmission and the emergency brake. The contracting foot brake works on the driveshaft. The bell, on the left, is operated in the simplest possible way—via a rope attached to the clapper.

15

American La France

This firm, as indicated in the Ahrens-Fox section, can trace its roots to the company founded by Chris Ahrens. His organization ultimately became a part of the American Fire Engine Company, and when this establishment combined with the company founded by Truckson La France—another pioneer of steam-powered fire engines—the American La France company was the result. The new organization chose Elmira, New York, home of La France, as its base of operation.

American La France began manufacturing gasoline-powered fire engines in 1910, at first using the Simplex chassis, propelled by a four-cylinder unit. By 1911 the company designed and manufactured its own six-cylinder engine. This unit was mounted in a new chassis, also of in-house construction. The following two decades saw further additions to the line but, although the catalog listed both centrifugal and piston pumps, the overwhelming majority of apparatus built by the company consisted of rotary gear pumps.

In 1931, American La France confirmed its position as one of the leaders in the industry by introducing a new V-12 engine. This impressive unit powered not only the company's flag-ship fire engines for three decades, but was also used in trucks, boats, buses and locomotives. American La France—truly a pioneer—is still in business today.

The example featured on these pages is from 1921, and represents a collaboration between La France and Brockway, the truck manufacturer. The exquisitely restored survivor is on permanent display at the Hall of Flame.

The American La France featured here is not equipped with a pump. It instead sports two Champion-style chemical tanks, each containing 35 gal of water. The interior of these tanks hold bronze bottles filled with sulphuric acid. When preparing the contraption for operation, one would turn the tank—which rotates—upside-down, at which point the acid would mix with the water to form carbon dioxide gas. Thus fortified, the water would be pressurized at a rate of about 80 psi. Each tank would last for about five minutes. Obviously, this type of fire-fighting apparatus was not suited for the big cities, but was adequate for smaller rural departments. The popularity of the chemical engine reached a peak during the horse-drawn era. By the early twenties, it was in fact vanishing.

Previous page

After the 1931 introduction of its V-12 engine, American La France further consolidated a position of leadership by the 1938 unveiling of a new body style—shown on the previous spread. In this photograph the intriguing lines have been accentuated by the use of a wide-angle lens. The new look was so advanced that it immediately made the products of other manufacturers seem dated. The streamlining of the Series 500, as the new model was called, began with a wide, smooth nose and swept back via bold, round fenders to the ultimate enclosure of both the hard suction hoses and the overhead ladder.

The Series 500 featured here—a 1940 model—was procured new by the fire department in Gilroy, California. It enjoyed uninterrupted service until a few years ago, when it was finally retired to a new role as part of the attractions in the future Tree Haven theme park. Most examples of this model featured a siren mounted on the hood just ahead of the windshield. This unit, however, lacks the siren, and relies solely on a bell, which is located behind the grille and operated from the dashboard via a cable. The pump is mounted in the cowl, while the suction ports—one on each side—are located just behind the cockpit doors.

This photograph shows the business side of the American La France. The large gauge on the left side of the instrument panel measures the pressure (or the vacuum) at the intake side, while the gauge on the right shows the pressure on the pump side. The smallest of the gauges keeps track of the oil pressure, while the medium-size unit indicates the rpm. Below the panel one finds the hand throttle—in the middle—as well as governors connected with the pressure-relief system. In conjunction with the two chromed hose couplings one finds the two pertinent valve levers, which move up and down. Located between these is a handle operating a valve on the other side of the rig—this handle moves in and out. Scattered at the bottom, a collection of bleeder valves. The Series 500, with its advanced styling, was quite a sensation in its day. This particular example was in fact a part of the American La France display at the San Francisco World's Fair in 1939. A prominent Gilroy man purchased the rig right after the event and donated it to the local fire department.

Pictured above, the legendary American La France V-12 engine. Its surprise debut in 1931 was the result of a secret five-year development effort. The impressive machine actually consisted of two sixes joined together by a common crankshaft. The angle was unusually small— only 30 degrees, As much as 240 hp was extracted from the massive unit. Note the use of dual ignition systems—the theme of duplicity is carried through consistently, right down to the double sets of spark plugs.

The cockpit of the Series 500 American La France, to the right, features a total lack of sentimental styling gimmicks—it's all strictly business here. The large dial in the center of the dashboard is the speedometer. This, the medium-size dial immediately to the right (which is the oil pressure gauge), and the smallest dial (the fuel gauge) are original, while the rest are later additions.

Mack

Mack occupies a significant chapter in the history of commercial vehicles—a preeminence due not only to the pioneering role the company played in the trucking industry as a whole, but also to the legendary strength and durability of the products it built. Especially famous became the Mack Bulldog, introduced in 1915.

Although the company had built a few motorized ladder trucks in 1909 and 1910, the year 1911 marked the formal entry of Mack into the field of fire engine manufacture. Later with the coming of the Bulldog, Mack developed its own production pumping engine—first demonstrated in 1919—and the rugged combination worked its way into the hearts of fire fighters across the country, constituting the beginning of relationships that, in many cases, have lasted to this day.

The following decades saw a continuous development of the Mack fire apparatus. Notable designs were such firsts as the parallel-series pressure-volume pump in 1927, and the one-truck fire department unit in 1935. Product advance followed the general development cycles of Mack's line of commercial trucks. New fire engine models were introduced in 1938, 1954 and 1967. In 1957 Mack took over a cab-forward design developed by Ahrens-Fox. Improved by Mack engineers, this design turned into a significant new line for the marque. Throughout the years, the firm, based in Allentown, Pennsylvania, has continuously reaffirmed its position as a major manufacturer and innovator in the field.

The model featured here is from 1944 and was delivered to Paso Robles, California—a city it still calls home.

Pictured on this spread, the doorless cockpit of the city of Paso Robles' 1944 Mack. The faithful servant was for many years the first-responding unit, and it saw service until a few years ago, when it was finally deemed too valuable, as a reminder of times gone by, to risk in the everyday hustle and bustle of traffic and fire fighting. Now it is set aside for parade use only. According to the fire chief, everything still works perfectly—except for the glove-compartment latch.

Next page
The photograph on the following spread features the 1944 Mack displaying its massive might in front of the firehouse it has occupied since day one. Note the lack of chrome on a variety of details such as the front bumper. This was due to wartime restrictions on the use of chrome. In fact, the delivery of the unit as such was directly related to nearby Camp Roberts and the need to provide fire protection for this military installation. The Mack is equipped with a 500 gal tank, a 750 gpm pump, and 1,200 ft of 2½ inch hose. A single reel holds 150 ft of 1 inch hose for quick-attack applications.

31

Maxim

The Maxim Motor Company, located in Middleboro, Massachusetts, took up fire engine manufacture in 1914, when Carlton Maxim felt he could improve on the apparatus of the day and decided to build a hose car for the local fire department. This contraption rested on a Thomas Flier chassis, as did a pumper he constructed the following year. In 1916 Maxim built the first pumper on his own chassis. By 1918 the company offered a complete line of fire engines.

Maxim was able to weather the Great Depression thanks to the success of a new line of pumpers and ladder trucks introduced in 1931. These were powered by six-cylinder Hercules engines. The pumps were made by Hale Fire Pump Company. Enveloping this package was a new, attractive body style, which featured a distinctively rounded radiator cowling. Further streamlining was achieved in 1936 through the introduction of another new design.

Maxim entered the postwar era with an all-new line of quadruple pumpers and city service ladder trucks. This 1946 introduction meant a further consolidation of the company's position, again very much thanks to the distinctive styling, which remained a feature of Maxim rigs for the following 15 years. The example featured on these pages represents the first year of postwar production, and is also a Hall of Flame exhibit.

In 1959, the company introduced a cab-forward design, which was offered in conjunction with the conventional line. Maxim is still in operation today, but since the mid-fifties as a Seagrave subsidiary.

To the left, behind that distinctively styled nose hides a six-cylinder Hercules. The manufacturer of this type of engine, which specialized in power sources for industrial application, was a Maxim supplier for years. A feature that disappeared gradually during the postwar era, but was still incorporated in the Hercules design, was the double ignition setup. The Maxim is equipped with a 500 gpm centrifugal-type pump, manufactured by Hale Fire Pump Company.

The photograph on the following spread emphasizes the streamlined body of the 1946 Maxim, and illustrates the care the stylists have taken to enclose all parts of the apparatus (the door covering the discharge couplings was temporarily removed when the picture was taken). The unit is a triple combination, which means it carries pump, booster tank with 1,500 ft of hose, as well as ladders. The attractive unit was donated to the Hall of Flame by the fire department in Chesire, Connecticut, as the result of one of their fire fighters paying a visit to the museum.

Seagrave

Frederick Seagrave started building ladders in 1881. After ten years in Detroit, he moved to Columbus, Ohio, where his firm prospered into one of the leading manufacturers of hand- and horse-drawn wagons. The company unveiled its first self-propelled fire truck in 1907.

Seagrave soon established itself as an innovator. Such firsts as the automatic pressure regulator, introduced in 1912, and the self-contained auxiliary cooling system, introduced in 1915, were early links in a long chain of inventions. Seagrave had already from the beginning concentrated on the centrifugal-type pump, and ultimately had the satisfaction of seeing the complete acceptance of this system.

Seagrave introduced a major diversification of its line in 1923. The new marketing plan attempted to cater to both large and small fire departments. The latter were courted by the Suburbanite, featuring a 350 gpm pump. At the other end of the spectrum was the Metropolite, with a capacity of 1,300 gpm. In 1932, the company countered the threat posed by the American La France V-12, by introducing its own V-12.

By the mid-thirties, syling had become an important aspect of marketing, and Seagrave unveiled a new look in 1935. The distinctive sloping grille would stay virtually unchanged until 1951, which marked the introduction of an even more radical design—a look that would last for nearly two decades. The Seagrave name is still alive today.

The classic beauty featured on these pages is from 1926, and is the proud possession of the Northern California community of Morgan Hill.

The photographs on this and the following spread feature front and three-quarter views of the Seagrave purchased new by the Morgan Hill Fire Department in 1926. The handsome pumper saw service until 1956, when it was relegated to the position of water truck for the Department of Public Works. This assignment lasted about a decade, after which it was left to die a slow death stored away at the city's sewer plant. In 1974 the old faithful was rescued by Butch and Jim Xavier, fire-fighting brothers—the former a volunteer, the latter a captain. With the help of others in the department the two enthusiasts set out to give the Seagrave a ground-up restoration. They were aided in their attempts to return the rig to its original state by the fact that an inquiry at the Seagrave factory produced a photo of the unit taken the day it was delivered. Another photo is also on hand at the El Toro station in Morgan Hill, where the survivor lives today— this picture shows the Seagrave the way it looked before the restoration.

43

Featured here, a nostalgic look at the open-air cockpit of the 1926 Seagrave, complete with a view of its attractively spoked steering wheel as well as its luxuriously pleated leather seat. A closer examination of the dash reveals a speedometer of the roller type—in the dial to the right—and two smaller gauges, oil-pressure to the left, and ampere to the right. An examination of the floor, which, like all the woodwork is of oak, shows clutch and brake pedals equipped with curious antislip devices. Beside the dim-switch, which is located just to the right of the throttle pedal, can be seen the end of a wire—the temporary choke cable. The restorers are still searching for the original equipment. Another missing item is the bell. It has been traced to a local family, who unfortunately refuses to give it up. However, the restorers have traveled this far, overcoming a multitude of problems along the way, and hope for a solution to this dilemma as well.

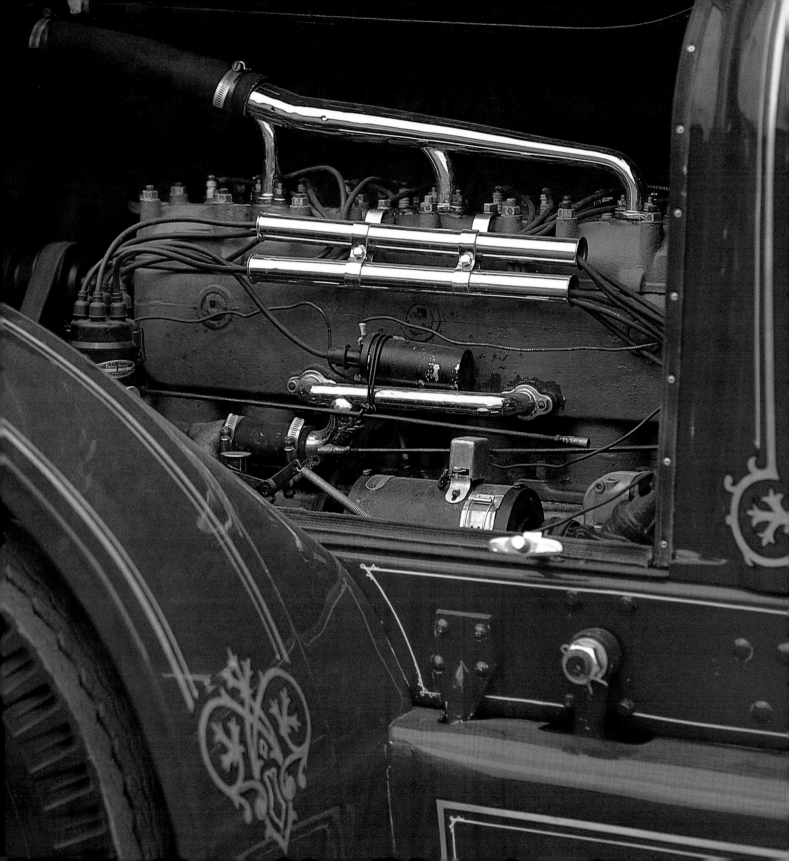

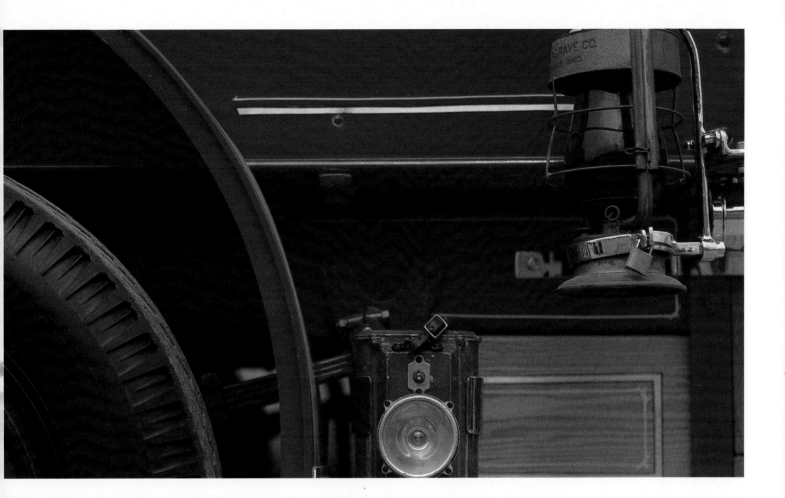

The Seagrave is powered by a straight-six Continental boasting a displacement of 331 ci, a bore and stroke of 3.75 × 5 inches, and an output of 70 hp. Note the dual ignition setup, with one system working off a magneto, and the other off a distributor. The engine was totally rebuilt. Parts were at first a problem, but when the restorers made contact with an enthusiast in nearby San Jose, the work began to move ahead at a decidedly faster pace.

The exact shade of color was arrived at by removing a chip of old paint from a spot that had not been exposed to the elements. This sample was then professionally matched by the paint manufacturer. The gold leaf work was applied by an old master who spent three days and three nights in the fire station performing his art. The Deitz Fire King kerosene lamp is original equipment, while the battle lamp is a later addition.

Next page
The following spread shows the Seagrave from the ladder side. The 12 ft unit is not the original one—it has long since disappeared. This particular rig came equipped with a 350 gpm pump. The water tank, located below the hose basket, holds 75 gal. The basket features a coil of 200 ft, 1 inch hose—black, as it was in those days. There is no telling how much this 60-year-old beauty is worth today, and it certainly will not come up for sale—but the price paid when new was $3,300.

The unit featured on these pages is a 1956 version, and came originally from the San Francisco Fire Department. It now rests in Garden Valley, California, where this and a 1957 companion saw service until 1986. The units were mainly used for structural fires and have 1,000 gpm pumps, 400 gal tanks and twin hose reels holding 150 ft each. To the left is the open-air cockpit with its rugged, utilitarian environment. Notice that the inside of the windshield has its own set of wipers.

Shown here, two views of the new styling introduced by Seagrave in 1951. This year marked the company's seventieth year, and the type is referred to as the Seventieth Anniversary Series. The photograph above illustrates the massive effect accomplished by the use of a boxy design for the various elements, such as hood and fenders. The long grille bars accentuated the width, and the center-mounted Federal siren brought to mind the streamlined locomotives with their intriguing-looking beacons.

Next page
The following spread shows the flowing profile of the Seventieth Anniversary Series Seagrave. Under that long hood hides the company's awesome V-12, which, with its 240 hp, produces more than enough power to propel the massive, tank-like fire fighter to appropriate speeds. The rear fenders were designed in such a way that a variety of compartments could be built in. They also served as stepping platforms. The last of these impressive Seagrave giants were delivered in the early seventies.

53

Pirsch

The Nicholas Pirsch Wagon and Carriage Plant of Kenosha, Wisconsin, was founded in 1857. When son Peter took over the leadership of the firm, the name was changed to Peter Pirsch & Sons. For many years the company built hook-and-ladder wagons. Its entry into the field of self-propelled fire engines came relatively late—the first pumper was built in 1916.

The company's specialization in ladders is evidenced by an awesome 100 ft straight-frame aerial delivered already in 1920. In 1926 Pirsch designed its own fire engine chassis but, unlike most of the other major fire apparatus manufacturers, the company never built its own engines. Power as a rule came from the Waukesha six-cylinder fire service engine. In 1931 Pirsch introduced a patented hydro-mechanical aerial. In 1935 the company built the first 100 ft all-power unit.

While reinforcing its leadership in ladder technology, Pirsch continued to build fire engines. These had received a very attractive new radiator design in 1935. The look was further refined in 1938, and by 1940 another facelift introduced the tall and narrow grille that would characterize the marque until the last deliveries of the engine-forward models in the early seventies. At this time the mainstay of the company's pumpers were of the cab-forward design, introduced in 1962. Pirsch is still in business today.

The example featured on these pages is a most fitting representative of Pirsch panache. It is a 1937 tractor, coupled to an 85 ft aerial, and marketed as the Pirsch Senior Model.

57

Previous page
Featured in all its might on the previous spread is the pride of Kenosha. The city is the home of the Pirsch company, and the fire department naturally favored the local son in its choice of equipment. The department used the impressive rig until 1969, when it was donated to the Hall of Flame. The museum's curator, Peter Molloy, has donned an appropriate fire-fighter uniform for a short stint behind the wheel. Not only was the radiator design distinctively Pirsch, but the triangular frame that supported both the bell and the Mars warning light became something of a trademark. Note the huge siren mounted below the bell—no chance of this rig passing unheard. Pictured on this spread, the scene at the end of the rig, where the tillerman reigns supreme, high atop the tall stack of ladders. John McLean enjoys the view from up there. The tillerman's cockpit is protected by its own windshield and canvas fairing.

60

To each his own

The fire apparatus industry flourished fabulously in the early part of the twentieth century. As it became obvious that the days of the horse were numbered, many an entrepreneur saw a bright future in outfitting the fire departments of the nation with the new self-propelled monsters. Thus begun the specialized field of fire engine manufacture. Some of these ventures failed, while others succeeded. By the early twenties the scene was dominated by American La France, Seagrave and Ahrens-Fox. Other manufacturers also enjoyed healthy market shares, such as Maxim, Mack, Pirsch and Stutz.

As has already been mentioned, Ahrens-Fox never really recovered after the Great Depression, and finally succumbed in the fifties. The great Stutz didn't even last that long. Other initially successful builders of fire engines who ultimately went the same way were Buffalo, General and Boyer.

But the big rigs with their capacity pumps and ladders were mainly applicable to the needs of the big cities. There was, however, a large market to be found in the smaller cities and the rural towns with their volunteer departments. Many a manufacturer saw this as their venue, and specialized in building fire apparatus applied to stock vehicles—some firms even offered kits that could be adapted to any old truck. One of the most popular marques for this application was the Ford, beginning with the T and moving along to the A and its potent V-8 configuration.

The example shown on this and the following spread is a 1935 Ford, fitted with Pirsch apparatus, and now the proud parade vehicle of the Hall of Flame.

This 1935 Ford was equipped by Pirsch and sports a rotary pump of Hale manufacture. Capacity is 500 gpm. The triple-combination pumper has a 100 gal booster tank and 1,200 ft of hose. The lever mounted on the outside of the driver's compartment, as in the photograph on this spread, engages and disengages the clutch for pumping mode. There is also a neutral position. A closer look at the panel under the seat reveals a valve which manually controls a pressure-relief system. The attractive rig was donated by the fire department in Slinger, Wisconsin, and subsequently restored by the Hall of Flame museum, which has a well-equipped restoration shop. This branch of the operation is presently run by Don Hale, a veteran enthusiast and restorer. The Ford was invited to take part in the parade celebrating this 100 year anniversary of Phoenix in 1986.

The skillfully restored old pumper shown on this and the following spread also comes from the rich and varied collection of the Hall of Flame museum. The Model T Ford dates from 1920 and has a unique background in that it was part of a 200 unit order placed with the Howe Fire Apparatus Company of Anderson, Indiana, by the US Army. The photograph on this spread affords a panoramic view of the mid-ship-mounted pump, which is of a three-cylinder piston type. The impressive contraption is driven from a jackshaft and power is transmitted, as can be seen here via a chain. Capacity is 300 gpm, and the booster tank—located on the other side of the pump—contains 25 gal. The reel holds 150 ft of 1 inch hose. As can be seen in the photograph on the following spread, the hood, headlights and fenders are standard Ford fare. Note that the hard suction hose—twisting like a huge anaconda—is carried across the hood, as was often the style in those days.

This spread features another of the unique little items found in the Hall of Flame—a 1946 Willys Jeep turned fire truck. The conversion is the work of Howe, then operating out of Anderson, Indiana, now located in Roanoke, Virginia. The pump is of the centrifugal type and manufactured by Barton-American of Battle Creek, Michigan. Capacity is 400 gpm. The Willys is normally pulling a trailer (missing in this picture) which holds a 250 gal tank and 75 ft reel of 1 inch hose. When in fully operational condition, the system depends on two hose and pipe connections to the trailer. One runs from the tank to the pump; another from the pump to the hose. The hard suction hoses are carried on top of the risers. The Willys was perfect for fighting grass fires, and served the volunteer fire department in Lake Geneva, Wisconsin, with distinction. The competent little rig is now on loan to the museum from the personal collection of founder George F. Getz, Jr.

The rig featured on this and the previous spread, a 1950 Autocar—powered by a six-cylinder engine designed and built in-house—represents a unique and interesting development from a fire apparatus viewpoint. The installation was done by the Edgar Tank Works of Linden, New Jersey, and features a high-pressure fog unit—a system developed by the US Navy during World War II. The system is powered by a Hardie triplex-type piston pump that develops as much as 600 psi, but puts out just 60 gpm. The result is a fine mist which—inside a burning building, for instance—starves the air of oxygen and puts out the fire with a minimum of water damage. The rig is not equipped to suction from a pond or other such source, but can only be supplied from a hydrant—with the small amounts of water used, the 500 gal tank goes a long way. Pictured on this spread, the impressive cockpit of the Autocar. The three levers on the floor are, on either side, the gear shifter and the emergency brake. Between them, the lever that engages the pump.

Vanishing breed

Few things in life are for free—received for free, given for free, done for free. Yet, there exists this more-or-less visible world of the volunteer. He or she constitutes a vital force on many levels of society—in politics, in health care, in charity and, as it pertains to this book, in fire fighting. There sometimes seems to be no limit to what people are willing to do to satisfy a need, within society, within themselves—or both. But even a volunteer fire fighter, as the system is functioning in most such departments, does receive some remuneration, although minimal.

There are, however, the vanishing few pockets where absolutely nothing is received. If money does change hands, it goes the other way—it is given, to support the department. One such pocket is found in the small town of San Miguel—population around 600—located in central California, far from everything, except dry, yellowing grass. The main street runs parallel to the railroad tracks, but the trains are not stopping anymore. Neither are the automobiles speeding by on the highway— the gas stations have all turned into monuments of a vanishing culture.

In this picturesque little place there are no less than 17 regular fire fighters, plus 16 auxiliary ones. All of them, from the chief down, are unpaid volunteers. The department has four rigs—the oldest, and its pride and joy, is a 1937 International, used mainly for parades. Another is the 1946 Reo, which, complete with its number-one driver, Linda McClure, decorates this spread.

This 1946 Reo was, when its time for retirement arrived, procured from the California Department of Forestry in King City. Fortunately, retirement in this case meant a new lease on life, and the faithful fire fighter has now served San Miguel for a good number of years—and is still going strong. The Reo is especially well suited for the needs of the community, thanks to the fact that the rig is equipped with a pump that is powered by its own engine—a Hercules, producing 350 gpm. This feature makes it possible for the truck to roll while pumping, which is a great advantage when fighting grass fires—the most common type of emergency handled by the department. The photograph on the following spread shows a sideview of the handsome unit. Its six-cylinder engine transmits power to the wheels through a five-speed transmission, and can be further moderated by a two-speed rear end. Running the Reo at full speed, which means well over 70, is quite a handful, says Linda McClure, who does not complain about the lack of power steering, however.

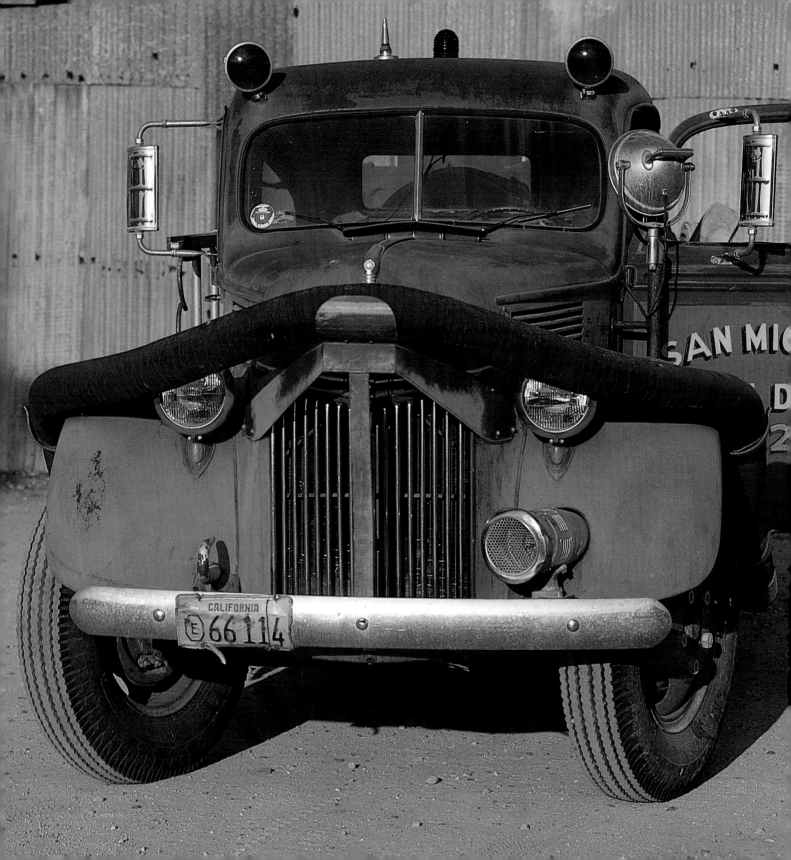

The faded face of the survivor featured on this spread is a tribute to the old saying: "If it ain't broke, don't fix it." After a closer look at the old-timer—a 1940 Ford V-8—one is tempted to take the word play one step further and say: "Don't fix it, even if it's broke." Well, all the essentials are in working order. Sure, the siren is dented—but it works. And the horn button is cracked—but it works. True, the tach doesn't work, but who needs it anyway? A trained ear immediately recognizes the appropriate engine speed.

The photograph above reveals more of the charming old body of this workhorse, which is a unit still in use at the San Miguel volunteer fire department. For maximum readiness the rig is kept in the driveway of the particular fire fighter on call. Despite its run-down appearance, the Ford performed with valor during a recent grass fire, which took it as far away from home as 27 miles. Normally, the primary purpose of this rig is to fight structure fires.

Next page
The caretaker of the old Ford is Gib Buckman, who has a sentimental reason for his attachment—his father bought the rig when Gib was six years old. The pump is by Van Pelt, of Oakdale, California. And it is an early one—number 305 built. It produces 500 gpm. The tank contains 250 gal. And there is 1,000 ft of 2½ inch hose on board. Buckman may look as bored as the Maytag Man, but when the buzzer goes off, both Gib and the Ford—pictured on the following spread—know perfectly well what to do.

The Ford has never seen paint during its nearly half a decade of existence, according to Buckman, not to speak of polish—and the bird's-eye view above is ample evidence. Well, the paint may be shot, but take a look at the chrome strip on the hood—they sure don't make chrome like that anymore. "This rig gets me a lot of smart remarks," says Buckman with a grin. "Once, when I pulled out of my driveway, some guy asked me if I was going to a parade. 'No,' I said, 'I'm going to a fire.'"

Pictured to the right, the sumptuous interior of the Ford. There is no telling how far the old workhorse has traveled. "The gauge broke 20 years ago," says Buckman. Note that only one of the windshield wipers has rubber—the one on the driver's side. "But the old flathead is strong and healthy like a young horse," he continues. "And come to think of it, that thing has never been rebuilt. Not in almost 50 years."

Beyond the classics

The classic fire engine featured the motor up front, which resulted in the long-hooded look of the era. During its heyday, in the thirties, the Ahrens-Foxes were as long as you could wish for—thanks to that glorious front-mounted piston pump. The biggest American La Frances of the early thirties also looked impressive with their squared-off, multilouvered hoods.

In the mid-thirties the arrival of streamlining made the enclosed cab a fashionable feature. The period also saw interesting odd arrangements, such as some of the units built by the General Fire Truck Corporation of Detroit in the late thirties, which combined both the long hood—necessarily so because of the straight-eight Packard engine it enclosed—and the streamlined cab, which actually came from a Ford club coupe.

In 1939, American La France introduced the cab-forward concept, which was further refined after the war, and this style soon became the only type offered by that manufacturer. Other companies developed their own cab-forwards, but usually offered the engine-forward design as well. Thus the old style hung on for a couple of decades, but all manufacturers ultimately switched to the new design. This unfortunately meant an end to the classically long hoods.

The photograph on this spread shows a typical representative of modern fire engine design, captured in smoke-filled action on a southern California freeway. The Redlands-based unit is a 1981 model, built by Crown Coach Corporation, of Los Angeles. Power comes from a Cummins diesel. The pump is a 1,500 gpm Waterous.

The photograph on this spread features a 1964 Van Pelt belonging to the volunteer fire department in Arroyo Grande, California. The triple-combination engine is equipped with a 1,000 gpm Hale centrifugal pump, a 500 gal tank, 2,000 ft of hose and the basic 35 ft and 28 ft ground ladders. On this particular day the services of the Van Pelt was called for in connection with combatting a grass and windbreaker fire, which, fueled by strong winds—there were gusts of up to 30 mph—turned into a major undertaking. It took 16 engines from six different agencies ten hours to contain the blaze. The Van Pelt, which has now entered its third decade of service to the community, is soon due to be replaced by a brand-new 75 ft Tele Squirt, also by Van Pelt. The department prefers to stay with the same manufacturer for all its equipment, in order to maintain coordination of operating panels and parts.

91

Previous page
Featured in action on the previous
spread, a 1986 Ford cab-over,
outfitted by Western States, of
Cornelius, Oregon. The unit is
equipped with a 1,250 gpm Waterous
pump. The tank holds 650 gal.
There is 1,800 ft of 2 ½ inch hose
and a 24 ft extension ladder carried
on board. The roof-mounted
cannon is an Akron with a Taskforce
master stream nozzle, putting out as
much as 850 gpm. The unit is
stationed in Nipoma, California. On
this spread, posed against a
dramatically smoke-yellowed sky, a
1973 International, equipped by Van
Pelt and powered by a Caterpillar
diesel. The Hale single-stage
centrifugal pump puts out 1,250
gpm. The tank holds 800 gal;
perhaps this huge volume is related
to the large number of discharges
featured on the unit—no less than
five 2 ½ inch (two on each side and
one at the stern), two 1 ½ inch (at
the stern), one 1 inch (on the
starboard side of the stern), and one
¾ inch (at the stern). A cannon can
shoot at targets as far as 200 ft away.
The well-equipped rig belongs to
the volunteer fire department in
Grover City, California.

Historic highway

There are few places like the Mother Lode country in California. After all, this is where it all began—this is where gold was discovered. And although there must be hundreds of counties and communities in the nation where one could presumably embark on informal fire engine discovery tours, the California Gold Country holds an intrigue all its own.

A carefully planned and perfectly scientific journey to study the area from the viewpoint of fire-fighting nostalgia, should probably have started in Nevada City or Auburn, both historic spots located along Highway 49—the Golden Chain that ties the Mother Lode counties together. But for the purpose of the limited photographic report appearing on the following pages, the trip was begun in Diamond Springs, right in the heart of El Dorado County.

The excursion ended three days later in Columbus, an old gold rush town near the end of Highway 49, and the site of a beautiful historic park. During the first weekend in May, for 27 years now, this park has been the setting of a Muster put on by the Mother Lode Firemen's Association. The event has seen steady growth in popularity over the years, and today constitutes one of the best-attended events on the town's calendar.

The photograph on this spread shows one of the many fire engines that found their way to this year's Muster. The heavy-duty face with its distinctively shaped grille, belongs to a 1941 White. The rig is the proud property of the Colma Fire Department, a small community just south of San Francisco.

Sutter Creek was founded by John Sutter, the man who made the first California gold discovery. The town's main street is lined with historic buildings, many of them dating back to the 1860s. The small firehouse, seen to the left, also faces the main street, and has room for two units—out front is the 1960 Dodge equipped with Van Pelt apparatus. It boasts a 750 gpm pump and a 500 gal water tank, and is mainly used for structure work.

Diamond Springs was once a boom town and a stop along the Kit Carson immigrant trail. Today its mossy firehouse stands as a charming reminder of times past. Dale Lambert guards the volunteer department's 1941 Ford. He and his fire-fighter friends have restored the old-timer to better-than-new condition—or at least better than when the department got it as surplus after World War II. The Ford, which was in service until 1977, has apparatus by Ward La France. The pump is by Waterous and produces 500 gpm. The water tank holds 150 gal. Nowdays the rig is only used for parade work.

Although it is difficult to imagine today, the town of Volcano was once home to 5,000 miners. It even had its own public library in those days, the first community in California to offer this convenience. Another first was a literary society and a little theater movement. Today the population is less than 100—and who knows how many are miners. The original settlers thought the small valley might have once been a crater, but there is no volcano in Volcano, never was—but there is an old fire truck Volcano, a 1949 GMC. At the time the photographs were snapped, there was no one around to tell how much action the old-timer is seeing these days, but one should certainly be careful not to put too much weight on the steps of the old ladder.

This charming little firehouse—
which also doubles as city hall and
library—is certainly befitting the
nation's smallest incorporated
city—Amador City. Founded in
1848 by Jose Amador, the town did
not see any gold to speak of until
1861, when a huge vein of gold-
bearing quartz was discovered. The
claim was exhausted in the early
part of the century, and Amador
City gradually reverted to what it
once was—not much more than a
bend in the road. In the photographs
on this spread the firehouse is
flanked by the massive trees that
grow in front of the grand old
Imperial Hotel. Peeking through the
open door of the firehouse, which
sits on top of a creek that runs
through the town, is the 1964
International, built by the now
defunct Maynard Fire Apparatus
Company of Marshfield,
Massachusetts. The centrifugal
pump produces 350 gpm.
Fortunately the aging International
does not see much action—a thick
layer of dust had to be removed
before the rig would match the red
of the door.

It is early Saturday morning in Mokelumne Hill, and the town's fire engine gets a shakedown. The firehouse—on the right—was built in the forties. Most of the buildings in Mokelumne Hill are older, but none are as old as the original settlement—as was the case with many a boom town, a devastating fire burned it to the ground. And that is perhaps why Mokelumne Hill has such an active fire department today. Although, the logic does not extend to other areas—the town that was once home to such infamous criminals as Black Bart, does not have a sheriff. The pride of the Mokelumne Hill Volunteer Fire Department, its 1950 GMC, although pretty old by now, has held up very well. Frank Reed, who lives behind the firehouse, and is the town's retired fire chief, says of the old faithful: "Best damned rig we ever had."

105

The pictures on this spread are ample proof of the pride the volunteers of the Mokelumne Hill Fire Department take in keeping their old faithful in tip-top condition. Although this particular morning the GMC does not show any signs of having been through hell—it stands as clean and shining as the day it came from the factory—it was only just recently that the rig had to be rushed through a 20 ft wall of flames to save it from being trapped during a violent grass fire.

Next page
The photograph on the following spread focuses on the broadly smiling face of the GMC. The unit was built by Van Pelt and has a front-mounted centrifugal pump, producing 250 gpm. The water tank holds 300 gal. There is 1,200 ft of 2 ½ inch and 300 ft of 1 inch hose on board. A 24 ft extension ladder, plus a 14 ft roof ladder, adds versatility to the well-equipped equipage. Volunteer fire fighters Roger Pittow and Richard Hurst stand at the ready on the running boards.

Pictured on this spread, an old-timer from the City of Angels—Angels Camp, a town founded by George Angel 75 years ago. This is the site of the celebrated annual frog-jumping contest, a tradition as old as the town, and first made famous by Mark Twain, who himself spent many a night at the Angels hotel. The fire department is also as old as the town, but has had only three chiefs—one of them, Chief Carley, served for 47 years, and was responsible for the purchase of the cheerful 1941 Dodge captured to the right.

The Dodge has Van Pelt apparatus, with a front-mounted centrifugal pump that produces 400 gpm. The water tank holds 225 gal. A slip-on tank adds another 75 gal. Note the large tachometer attached to the steering column in the picture above. The Dodge has been in the department since new, but it was not always yellow. In 1963, Chief Carley became aware of the fact that yellow is the color that shows up the best—consequently, the same yellow as used on road signs was prescribed for all units in the department.

In the old days of the hand pumper Muster referred to an event when the volunteer fire fighters in the community came together for a head count. The occasion was always a good excuse for a party—was back then, and still is today, when Muster has taken on the semblance of a fair. The scene depicted on this spread is from the Columbus State Historic Park and the annual Muster held at this site. Saturday morning sees the gathering of engines and enthusiasts. In this picture a beautiful 1927 American La France has just arrived from Manteca, California, and is getting the once-over from the crowd. The engine was bought new by the city. Fifty years later it again looks as it did back then, thanks to a lot of hard work. Saturday afternoon sees the staging of the fun and games—the Bucket Brigade, the Hose Cart Races and other such competitive events traditionally found where fire fighters get together. Sunday is the big day—the day when the assembled machinery is paraded down Main Street of old Columbia.

To the left, the clean engine of a 1924 American La France. The straight-six boasts three plugs per cylinder, and produces 120 hp at 1,000 rpm. Delivered new to the city of Stockton, California, the rig was last used in a big 1959 fire. The restoration began in 1961, and took four years. A recent test drive caused the demise of a connecting rod—Howard Schroeder just got it back together in time for the Muster. With this beauty, he and his fellow fire fighters in Stockton have done themselves proud.

The sight captured by the photograph above is an unsual one—a 1918 Cadillac fire engine conversion. One of the founding fathers of the city of Atwater, California, owned the Cadillac for a number of years. When the man finally decided to trade it in for a new model, the price quoted was so ridiculously low that he instead had it turned into a fire engine, which he subsequently donated to the city. The color scheme—red, black and gold—is the original combination.

Next page
Pictured on the following spread, a 1941 Seagrave. Ken Wollard, volunteer fire fighter from Diamond Springs, is the third owner of this classic. First owner was the city of Albany, California. More than 100 hours of polishing has returned luster to the paint, which is the original coat. Power comes from Seagrave's Pierce-Arrow-patterned V-12. Wollard has had no luck finding parts for this unit. Should something break—knock on wood—he would be in trouble. In spite of this, he did not hesitate to drive it the 75 miles to the Muster.

The sight of fire engines brings out
the enthusiast in all of us it seems,
regardless of age and persuasion.
For the older generation the lure
must be a blend of nostalgia and a
long-standing fascination with the
machinery. For the younger set it
must be the enjoyment of discovery,
an amazement perhaps at the
realization that man has indeed
accomplished spectacular feats of
engineering long before the
computer era. Well, true, some
enthusiasts may not have a complete
grasp of what's going on, except
that it's a lot of fun. The fellows in
the picture to the left, certainly old
enough to be able to reach
independent conclusions, have been
stopped in their tracks by an old
GMC pumper brought out by the
local fire department. What is this
gauge? 400? Couldn't be the
speedometer, could it?

Sleeping beauties

To a fire engine enthusiast the discovery of a rusty old machine found abandoned in a backyard or overgrown in a field is all at once thrilling and distressing and challenging.

He is thrilled because he wants to find out what year and model it is. (Perhaps this one is a long-lost favorite?) And he is distressed because he hates to see the elements destroy a valuable piece of history. (It should be covered with a tarp.) And he is challenged because he can always see possibilities. (This one would be a perfect object for the long winter evenings and how can I talk the owner into selling it and how much will it take to convince him?)

As a matter of fact, even though the derelicts can still be found, the discovery of an abandoned fire engine is a far less common occurence than finding cars, trucks and tractors, which are still in abundance.

But survivors can still be found. One man who always keeps his eyes open is John Yeager of Phoenix, Arizona—where the climate is favorable for derelicts. Yeager represents a large and growing number of collectors scattered across the nation. Along the perimeter of his fenced-in yard in downtown Phoenix sits an intriguing row of sleeping beauties—among them can be found two Seagraves and five American La Frances. This time-capsule countenance in the photograph on this spread belongs to a 1926 American La France. Yeager found the survivor in Fort Madison, Iowa. While repairing new trucks is his business, rebuilding old fire engines is his hobby— the only problem, says Yeager, is to find the time.

The tradition of decorating the fire apparatus with fancy designs is an old one, dating back to the days when the fire department was a sort of social hub of the community. The highlight of the season was the parade, and the hand pumper, which constituted the state of the art at the time, would be painted by artists who were extremely skilled and sought after for their abilities. The contraptions were often painted in secret and unveiled with great ceremony come parade day. While the social trends changed, the tradition of beautifying the fire apparatus continued, and was carried on even as the new era of motorized equipment arrived. Nowdays the tradition is fading and the skilled craftsmen are vanishing. The delicate operation of gold leaf application requires both skill and patience. The 22 karat glitter can be painted on, or applied in the form of sheets. The finished design is covered with a protecting laquer. The subject in the photograph on this spread is a very fine example of craftsmanship and illustrates the longevity of the materials as well— the Seagrave is from 1935.

The 1924 Seagrave featured in the pictures on this and the previous spread originally came from Santa Monica, California. Today, it is still in the same state, but finally at rest behind the old Rinconada store, located just east of Santa Margarita. This machine is the famous scaled-down version of the full-size Seagrave—called the Suburbanite. Note that Seagrave already used solid-disc wheels, a feature American La France would not introduce until the early thirties. The windshield is a later addition.

The Suburbanite was powered by a Continental. Its decorative cast-iron surfaces—faded by the passing of time—are displayed in the photograph to the right. The pump, which was mounted mid-ship, is of the centrifugal configuration and produced 350 gpm. The workings of the elements always add a particular patina, a fusion of shades no overnight paint job could accomplish. Although it is certainly pleasing to see a perfectly restored unit, the charm of a sleeping beauty is unquestionable.

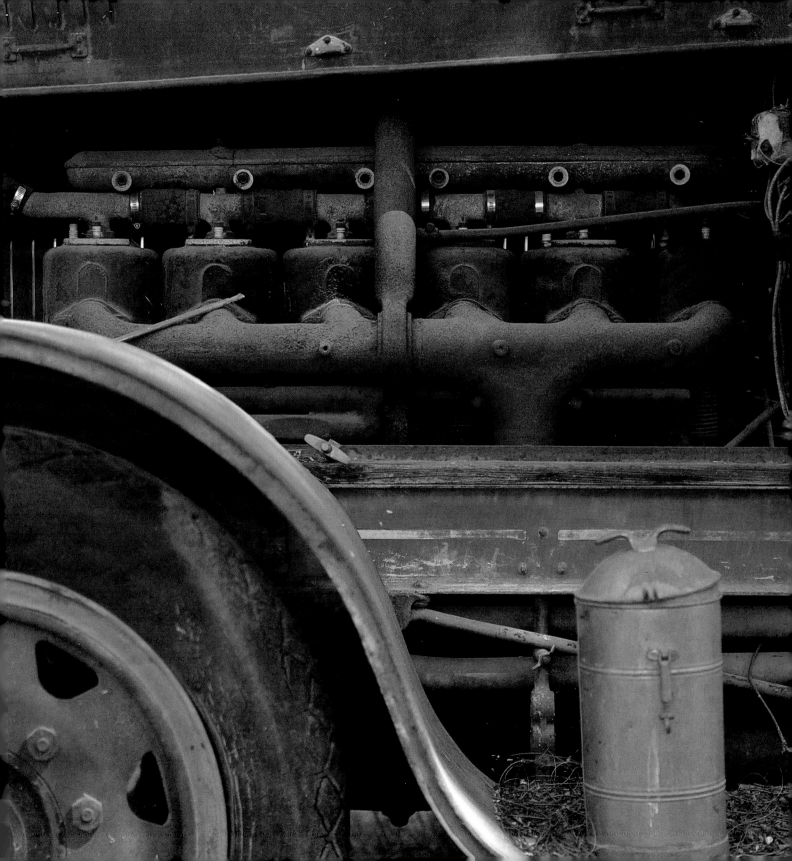

The fire-fighter helmet in the photograph above—made the old way, from leather—forms the vignette for the last page as well as for a note of appreciation to all the enthusiasts who made this book possible. A special mention should be given to Chris Cavette of the California Chapter of SPAAMFAA (Society for the Preservation and Appreciation of Antique Motor Fire Apparatus in America), for providing leads to owners of rigs; to Peter Molloy, curator of the Hall of Flame (the must-see museum operated by the National Historical Fire Foundation in Phoenix, Arizona), for his invaluable assistance; and, finally, to museum founder George F. Getz, Jr., for making available for photography so many of the treasured pieces in the collection.